21 Rules for New Magickal Students

Lady Tashi's Little Book of Magick

21 Rules for New Magickal Students

21 Rules for New Magickal Students

LADY TASHI

SKY GODDESS PRESS
An imprint of
DRAGON LADY MEDIA, LLC
SYRACUSE, NEW YORK
2020

First edition 2020

ISBN: 9798633781816

Printed by Amazon.com

Publisher:
Dragon Lady Media, LLC
Syracuse, New York 13209
publisher@cherylcosta.com

Dedication

To all the Witches, Mages, and Mystics, who wrote books
that gave me pieces of greater knowledge.

To all the Magickal and Mystical mentors of my life. Your
wisdom, insights, and heartfelt advice guided my path.

To my hundreds of Wicca and Mystical students.
Your questions were exit signs on the road to
greater understanding.

To the Lamas of the Tibetan Orthodox Tradition, who
taught me to tame my mind and listen to the song of the
Great Consciousness.

To All Witches, Past, Present and Future

CONTENTS

Table of Contents

Introduction

The reasons why people choose to study Metaphysics or the Magickal arts are varied and infinite. As a Craft teacher, I could not hope to give you all the reasons people want to study Witchcraft.

What I can do is define a loose structure of guidelines and rules that govern who I teach and under what conditions I allow a student to be under my tutelage. These guidelines vary among metaphysical teachers, but I can tell you that any magickal teacher worth their salt has a set of conditions under which they'll engage and maintain a student.

Within the magickal community, there are teachers and schools of Witchcraft and Metaphysics. Some of them are purely on a tutoring basis. Others are managed by local covens and circles. Still, others are governed by magickal clans and incorporated church organizations.

Some mystical groups are as well organized and structured

as an Ivey League College, others more like a small community college. Of course, there are magickal schools that are like a local vocational education operation, with loosely scheduled classes whenever teacher's personal schedules permit.

Each of these types of metaphysical organizations has rules. The degree of rigidity in terms of entrance requirements and academic standards varies with the kind of organization.

Then there is a level of a **personal tutor**. This is like studying with a local piano teacher who works out of their home. The teacher may have many students at different levels of experience; beginners, intermediates, and advanced students. This sort of teacher never really teaches mass classes but instructs on a one-on-one basis. The students are, in effect, Sorcerer's apprentices. <u>My rules are NOT coven level rules!</u> They are simply the rules and reasons that I set forth as a **personal tutor** magickal teacher.

For the record, Coven and Clan level rules are very different than those of a **personal tutor** like me.

In any case, all metaphysical teaching efforts are run by busy people with limited time, so most have rules. Rules that define what they expect from new and ongoing students. Are my rules absolute? Most the exclusivity rules have some case by case flexibility if the student is up front and honest about their situation; especially with regards to working with other teachers.

The rules in this book are my rules developed over forty

years of magickal practice. Sometime before this writing, I passed these rules along to several notable and experienced magickal adepts. Most of them concurred with my guidelines and the reasons for them. Some of these respected adepts would have liked to have added a few more rules.

These rules were developed to give you the best chance for success as you start your magickal spiritual journey.

As well they also help the teacher to not waste their time on students who aren't committed to the Magickal Art.

Respectfully,

Cheryl "Lady Tashi" Costa

Semi-Retired Priestess in Retreat

Rule 1

You come to the magickal arts of your own free will

So, the scenario goes like this, I'll be sitting in a coffee shop scribbling in my journal narrative, minding my own business. You, whoever you are, approaches and asked to speak to me. I invite you to join me in my booth. I offered to buy you a cup of coffee or tea. You tell me you would like to study the magical arts with me. I reply with some questions.

Why do you want to study magick and why are you asking me?

Why magick? It's a question about character. If you want to study for vague reasons, I'll tell you to go home and think it over and come back and see me in a few days. If I hear that you want to influence someone in love and affairs of the heart, I'll give you five dollars and tell you to go buy that special someone a lovely greeting card.

If I hear hostile inclinations, I'll say no and dismiss you

If I hear highly noble reasons, I'll most probably dismiss you too.

I'm not going to tell you what the right answer is!

If you've gotten this far, I'll press you on the question of why me? After you've done a great job of trying to flatter me up. I'll tell you; I am meaner than the nastiest coach you ever had in high school.

Hopefully, that will convince you that I'm not the teacher for you. Please understand I'm under absolutely no obligation to teach you the craft, none whatsoever.

If you try to butter me up and appeal to my ego, you're barking up the wrong tree.

You might get my attention if you engage me in a discussion about silly stuff. *"I mean why do people call it a hot water heater, I mean it's really a cold-water heater, isn't it?"*

If I detect a hint that you think I'm nuts. I will assure you that I'm crazier than the mad Hatter; and I'll suggest you seek another teacher.

On the other hand, if you dare to go into the silliness realm with me, I'll probably buy you another cup of whatever you are sipping. Why? Well, you just showed me a degree of flexibility and a willingness to stretch the bounds of your reality. The bottom line in the world of quantum mechanics and of magick; is that at times, it is seemingly silly, contrary, and very much counter intuitive.

The study of these topics requires your free will. You must choose to do magick not because you were born to it, drafted into it, or ordered to do it, or told to do so under duress. Example: You're only studying magick because your mom, dad, or girlfriend insisted. Wrong answer!

You must want this for yourself! You must come to this of your own free will, end of the story.

.

Rule 2

Study with whomever, but if you're studying with me it's my way or the highway

This is very straightforward.

It comes down to respect for your teacher. If you want to work with another teacher, that's all fine and dandy. Don't do so while you're under my tutelage. It's them or me. You shouldn't be wasting either my time or theirs.

I had a student once who asked several magical teachers to take her on as a student. Apparently, she had a laundry list of five or six teachers if memory serves. Two of us accepted her, not knowing of the other. Why did she do this? The best I can figure she thought teaching from two teachers would really give her the inside edge on the magical art.

The occasion of a Midsummer Festival came to pass. As it turned out, my counterpart teacher was hosting the main ritual at the festival. Amongst his student minions, helping with the ceremony was my student as a sub officiant in the rite. Afterward, I approached my peer teacher; I asked why the acolyte in question was helping him and his circle with the main ritual.

He told me she had been in his class for about six months. He indicated that she was a natural. I told him he had a very fine student and let it go at that. Later in the day, I ran into the acolyte and complimented her on her performance in the ceremony. She was visibly pleased with the compliment.

Then I reminded her about my rule of one teacher at a time. I politely told her she was better suited to the other teacher, and with that, I was dismissing her from my tutelage. The next morning, she was whining to friends about being dumped by me. Further, I heard that she had resorted to indulging in trashing me.

Had she bit the bullet and kept her peace, everything would have been fine. Her other teacher heard her trashing me and ask why. She told him I had dropped her from my program because of my one teacher rule. My peer was from a secret tradition and considered her taking lessons from me a violation of his trust. He unceremoniously dropped her from his cadre of students and dished out a considerable amount of chewing out as well.

At this point, she was out in the cold from two magickal teachers. With bad news traveling fast she found every teacher's door closed to her. She humbly came to me about two or three months later and told me she wanted to study with me again; which leads us to rule three.

Rule 3

You have my perfect love and perfect trust until you violate it

In Rule 2, I illustrated one young lady who broke my rule about being a student of two magical teachers at the same time.

Several months after both teachers booted her, she came to me hat in hand; apologized and graveled a bit. Finally, she begged to be reinstated as a student.

I told her to give me the night to sleep on it. After she left, I called my peer, the other teacher, and queried if she had approached him for reinstatement. As it turns out, she had! My peer turned her down, cold. I asked him if he planned to reconsider his answer was, "…no way José…"

I asked for his opinion about reinstating her. I pointed out that she had talent. He agreed that she had ability but not the discipline and maturity. I told him she'd have to prove herself both worthy and mature enough to deserve a second chance to study. In the back of my mind, I wondered if she was going to have a hissy fit when I told her the conditions.

I invited her to my favorite coffee shop for brunch the following Sunday. Over brunch I pointed out the degree of trust trouble she had caused. Again, she apologized. I told her it wasn't that simple.

I told her she could come back and be reinstated with the caveat.

The class was too far along, so she couldn't rejoin the current Class for beginners. I told her she was welcome to join the next class that started seven months in the future, she looked upset. I explained that she had some atonement to do. I told her that for the next seven months, she had to do a couple of things.

Each member of my magical clan always brought food to the monthly rituals. She would act as hostess, accepting the food offerings, and setting up a spread for the feast and cleaning up afterward.

Also, I pointed out that her bread making during the early stages of class before she was booted was subpar. I insisted on a weekly loaf of bread just as if she was in her old class. She was told she had to master her bread skills, as well.

Surprisingly she agreed to these terms! I had half expected a hissy fit and her stepping out the door. But she sucked it up and agreed to the conditions.

She did an excellent job with her atonement duties and

joined the next beginner's class, happily a year later.

I'm happy to report that she became a first-class witch and an excellent coven mother with her own students much later.

Her corporate job took her to the West Coast, and I'm sad to say I haven't heard from her in years. Perhaps, in another lifetime.

Rule 4

Your heart and responsibility must be 100% into your magick or go home

Let us be straightforward about this, NOT ALL PAGANS ARE WICCANS and NOT ALL WITCHES ARE WICCAN! I must be very clear about this. In fact, too many are just exploring or are in it for the party and the loose rules.

Many pagans, if you corner them about their theology, you'll get a grocery list of what they say they practice. Or they just tell you their eclectic, a buzz word for, a little bit of this, and a little bit of that.

Most pagans that I have met will not claim the witch title. It's a position they presume will keep them pleasantly safe from dogmatic ridicule.

Witches and Wiccans, on the other hand, tend to claim the title **Witch**, with all of its baggage.

They make commitments, whether it's a solitary practitioner or as a coven - circle member. In essence, when a witch makes their initiation bond with the Goddess, <u>they are, in effect, taking the vows</u>.

Many years ago, I was doing business with a witch I will call Lady A.

I wanted to do business with her, but I was up against several pagan folks with more experience. In the end, she took my humble product and contract. Later she pointed out that she prefers to do business with witches because of their ethics and vows.

Bottom line: Don't expect serious training in the magical arts if you aren't willing to make certain deep heartfelt commitments.

Understand this: I'm not asking you for your soul, I'm asking you for your <u>focus</u>, <u>your word</u>, and <u>your honor</u>.

Rule 5

The more magick you know, the less you use.

This is the hard rule to communicate to newbies and to non-magickal folks.

Mundane Example: I have a tool, an ax for chopping wood.

Do I use the ax for cooking?   No?   I don't.

Do I use the ax to do maintenance work in my car?
         Not in your dreams.

Do I use an ax to do the laundry?   Absolutely not.

It's like my high school industrial arts teacher used to say: ***"Use the right tool for the right job!"***

Magick isn't like the television show where somebody twitches their nose, and supper appears.

Magick isn't like a movie where someone hauls out an ancient-book-of-spells and finds one for every purpose.

Magick is about moving subtle forces in the universe to effectively manipulate the causes for a particular outcome.

Magick is about manipulating the machine code of reality to gently bend it for certain outcomes.

I used to teach a kid who initially thought using magick would fulfill his consumer desires. Think of it like this week he wanted a new video game, next week a surfboard and on and on. He was never satisfied with what he had, and it reflected in his magick. He treated magick like a personal vending machine. He didn't get all these things because his intentions were continually changing, and he literally couldn't maintain focus and keep his eyes on the ball. You can't approach magick as a free gift machine.

If you only have so much money, if you're smart, you'll get one thing that you really need. Notice I didn't say want.

Magick seems to work better when the goal is heartfelt-need versus a selfish-frivolous-want. Magick seems to work best when the goal is heartfelt generosity toward someone else's need.

Also, I have found that smart adepts sit on the unlimited potential of the magick and save the resource for a rainy day. I know that I said magick is an infinite resource, it is. But you are not an endless resource. The control of magick has to come from you. Magick is not about making a wish and then go play basketball.

Good magick focus is required meditation and a single-minded intention. Buddhists call it <u>mindfulness</u>.

Most people have scattered minds what Buddhists call "monkey chatter thoughts." If you have a monkey chatter mind, magick will be very difficult if not nearly impossible. This is why we meditate, to learn to calm our mental chatter, and to help bring about focus.

So, the more Magick you know, the less you use. Because it's a lot of discipline and a lot of work!

Rule 6

Magick is about heart, get your damned ego out of it

Over the years, I've known many new students who wanted to feel the exhilaration of working a piece of verifiable magick. Shortly after they do! They tend to get all cocky and present what I call the **"Great and Powerful Oz syndrome."** They develop an attitude like "I can do anything!"

Trust me, we've all been there, me included. Why do beginner's initial magick work and follow-on magick fall apart?

It's simple, really. Beginners start unsure of themselves. They usually approach magick with the innocence of a child, which is good. It's a humble, heartfelt drive to make it right and make it happen. As long as the magick is sincere and innocent, the magick works.

Once you start thinking you are all-powerful and your ego gets wrapped around the flagpole, losing your innocence along the way, the results of the conjuring go to pot, plain and simple.

That's why I use the baking of bread as a proxy tool in magickal training.

Bread making requires a relaxed manner and focus. Yes, you can make bread as a class master, as long as you keep your grade school focus and innocence during the effort. Start- getting sloppy, cut corners, and the bread will look like hell.

Magick like bread making requires focus, ethical practice, loving attention, and heart. Without heart there is no pride in your effort. An ego attitude – "I'm the best bread maker around, is not heart; the same goes for magic.

The heart requires a degree of innocence and humility. If your bread is first-class other people will talk up your product; the same goes for magick.

The heart is the key.

Rule 7

- We make bread to teach magick. You'll learn to make the bread or go home

This is a most essential point of contention. Over the years, I have offered many; introduction to magick classes. I've also had up to 10% of the class get up and stomp out when I explained that our first magical spell lesson was going to be making a <u>simple loaf of white bread</u>. Usually, as they left, they were muttering, "that's not real magick" or "making bread is stupid."

This, I suppose, was the first level of class cutting. As my track coach used to say,

"There are always some know-it-all's who aren't going to do some of the training routines. Sorry, we can't use them. So be it."

Why bread?

Initially, it's an excellent metaphor for magical practice and mindset. If I tell you exactly what ingredients to purchase and you freely substitute something else, there is usually a disaster waiting to happen. If you don't pay attention to the specifications: temperature, and time your results will be dismal.

Some class members go home and have second thoughts about studying magick because the idea of bread making is "either stupid like the first 10% said when they exited" or they get the impression that this is going to be too messy because they think real magick is a lot of silly wand-waving, charging crystals and mystic incantations.

Nah, nah, nah, magick is about <u>following directions</u>, at least initially. Later on, it's about understanding and having a <u>firm grasp of the power of the symbology.</u>

Back to bread making! Finally, bread making is about motivation and the ability to accept project failure and try, try again. If you are of the ego mindset of walking away from one loaf of bread failure, then you don't have the temperament for magickal practice.

The Magickal Art is about harnessing the awesome powers of the multiverse and channeling them into manifestation.

In that context: I have little respect for magickal students who are <u>defeated by a little loaf of white bread</u>!

If you can't make the bread, you'll never make the magick!

WHY?

Someday, you may want to work with potions and tinctures. You'll need the attention to detail, respect for process, and patience; that bread making will teach you.

That's why!

I use bread as a teaching tool for several reasons.

First, the bread dough is a great symbolic metaphor for the way magick is affected by both attentive and sloppy practice.

Second, making bread helps the practitioner relax and focus on something other than themselves.

Third, it's fun!

Fourth, you can eat it, it's yummy.

I'm strict on this notion: "If you can't make the bread, you'll never make the magick."

Oh, I suppose, if you dabble long enough or take the dark path and use angry-hateful emotions to generate a manifestation, you'll have some results. Results one shouldn't be proud of.

Look at it this way, if you have never baked before.

I dare say if you attempted to bake a cake or make brownies from scratch, you'd probably fail. Most people do. I still haven't mastered either of them.

<u>Baking is an acquired skill, so it is with magick.</u>

So, let's consider spells. Suppose you find an "old" book of magical spells in some used bookstore.

In each of these spells is typically a list of odd substances or ingredients. Usually, these spell book recipes are accompanied by some incantation. Will it work?

I suppose it worked for the person who wrote the book. I doubt that it will work for you. First and foremost, old and even ancient spells and incantations are more or less <u>useless</u> to the modern practitioner, because the old symbolism have little or no modern meaning to the contemporary adept.

Here's the problem. Let us suppose the book was written by some British witch. Right off the bat we have cultural issues with the ingredients. An herb ingredient in England might be called by a completely different name here in North America. Materials in themselves have no inherent magickal quality. These materials are, in effect merely symbolic, and are used to help the practitioner visualize some feature or quality imagined in the substance.

At the core of the magickal practice is visualization, and symbols are an important and compelling way of visualizing.

Our goal is to establish a basic set of symbols amongst our student practitioners to teach the mechanics of magick.

Once a student adept clearly understands the basic mechanics, then the symbology issue becomes simpler.

Let's return to making a loaf of plain white bread.

First off, forget the idea of making another type of bread, at least initially. You have no idea how many of my witch-let's take an attitude, "Oh, I don't eat white sugar." or "I only eat whole wheat bread."

This exercise is not about what you'll eat, it's about whether you can master a basic loaf of white bread and that is all.

It never fails that a quarter of my students on the first try at making a simple loaf of white bread decide to add other ingredients because they obviously know better.

Instead of white sugar, they use brown sugar. Instead of plain ordinary flour, they use whole wheat flour. Of course, my favorite, they toss some fruit like raisins into the bread. The results are always disastrous.

You have no idea how hard this is for some people to stay on point and focus on the objective.

The objective is to not get fancy but simply master a humble loaf of white bread. ONLY after the basic white loaf is mastered three times in a row, do we move on to variations on the theme. As my track coach used to say, "Keep running that play until you get it, right kid.!"

Mistakes are ok; rarely do people get it the first time. Dealing with and accepting problems with the bread is an exercise in conquering your fat ego and taming it a bit.

The best magick is performed with childlike innocence and humility. The fundamental bread-making skill takes a little honing if you keep each preparatory and baking consideration that I teach you, in the back of your mind, you'll master it. Its also an exercise in Mindfulness.

Tools you'll need.

- A kitchen thermometer
- An oven thermometer
- Liquid measuring vessel
- Dry measure scoops
- Measuring spoons
- 8x4 bread pan, "metal preferred"

Ingredients

1 – Tablespoon of white sugar

1 – package of dry yeast (2 ¼ teaspoons) DO NOT USE
BREAD-MACHINE YEAST

1 ¼ cup of warm water. (100° to 112°)

3 cups of all-purpose flour – sifted optional and
recommended.

1/4 teaspoon of salt

Cooking Spray

Draw and mix warm and cold tap water, measure the
temperature of the stream with your kitchen thermometer.
When you have a stable 110°-112° for about 60 sec, collect
1 ¼ cups of water from the stream.

DO NOT MICROWAVE! (100° to 112°) No more than
115°; otherwise, you'll kill the yeast.

Mix your sugar and yeast into the water, set aside for about
ten minutes. I foamy froth should appear on the top of the

water. If not, give it another 5 minutes. If the foamy froth doesn't appear, the water was either too hot, and you killed the yeast, or the yeast was old and not active. **STOP**

Rinse out the measuring cup and draw your warm water again, re-add your sugar and yeast, and mix. Wait 10-15 minutes. If no foamy froth appears and if your water was spec at (100° to 112°), then go out and purchase some fresh yeast. Don't bother mixing it into the dry goods, it won't work, and it's just a waste of materials. Go out and purchase some fresh yeast!

Let's assume you had a nice foamy froth on your water, sugar, and yeast mixture.

Measure 3 cups of flour into a large mixing bowl, add in your ¼ teaspoon of salt.

Mix into your good-looking foamy, froth water, sugar, and yeast mixture. Stir with a large wooden or plastic spoon until a soft dough begins to form.

Sprinkle some flour on a large clean cutting board or a clean tabletop.

Wash your hands, dry, and spray some cooking spray on your hands.

Remove the dough from the bowl and knead the dough until it becomes smooth with no chunks, and it becomes relatively elastic. Do not become too concerned if the bread-dough is a bit dry at first. The kneading action will distribute the needed moisture evenly within the mixture.

If by chance, it's very dry, you can add water by sprinkling a few drops on the dough and working them in. NOTE I said, a few drops!

After the first kneading, cover the bowl with a CLEAN damp towel and place it in a warm place without drafts and allow the dough to rise for 30-45 minutes.

This is a good time to pre-heat your oven to 350°F. Use your OVEN thermometer to monitor the actual temperature of the oven versus what the dial or read out says. Most ovens are 25°-50°F off one way other than the dial setting. Always use an oven thermometer to get it right! NEVER set the temperature and toss the bread into an oven coming up to temperature. You won't like the results. Pre-heat and once stable. Then and only then place the bread dough in the oven.

Last thought, the preheating oven helps make the room nice and warm to help the dough rise.

After the first rise, you will punch down the dough and allow it to rise again for perhaps 30 minutes. After the 2nd rise, spray the bread pan with cooking spray; take the dough out roll and fold the dough into loaf roughly the size of the 8x4 bread pan. Place the dough in the bread pan, and optionally you can lightly spray a little cooking spray on the bread. Cover the bread pan and dough with that warm damp towel and allow the bread to rise.

After about another 20-30 minutes, the dough if it's in a warm place will rise to nearly double in volume. Carefully remove the towel and place the bread pan in the oven.

(I recommend that the warm place not be on top of the warm stove, the dough will get overheated and start baking, Nah, Nah!)

We bake for about 30-40 minutes at 350°F – typically about 35 minutes. Remember, <u>each loaf is different</u>, and <u>each oven is different</u>. This is a judgment call. At 30 minutes, reach in and stick a long toothpick into the top of the bread, it comes back with dough sticking to it, give it more time. If it's clean and the bread is browned to your liking, remove and allow it to cool.

After about 20-30 minutes – gently dump the bread out onto a clean kitchen towel and place it on a wire cooling rack. After about an hour, feel free to slice off the end of the loaf. Look at the core of the bread; is it fully cooked or still doughy? If the bread is fully cooked, you got the time and temperature right.

If it's still doughy, give it 10-15 minutes more time the <u>next time you make a loaf</u>.

Rule: do not adjust the temperature and the time together next time. Increase one or the other, <u>but not both</u>. My experience suggests keeping the temperature stable and adding more time.

There, my witch friends, you have your **_first spell_** and your first magickal working.

Bread is life! Eat and enjoy it. In future lessons, I will explain how to use bread as a vessel for magickal working.

Remember: A magickal workings requires the same attention to detail, fussing, and planning. If it were easy, everyone would be doing it!

Failure Analysis

If the loaf failed, do a postmortem and examine every step you did.

Where you cheap, Charlie? And did not purchase a kitchen or oven thermometer? I bet you spent more money on a beautiful crystal Wand or a fancy Athame! The right tool for the right job! You can't guess these things; your hand is a horrible thermometer for water temperature testing.

Was the yeast too weak or too old? Was the water too hot or too cold?

Did you use whole wheat flour instead of all-purpose flour or bread making flour?

OH MY, did the dough overflow the bread pan and drip like stalagmites into the bottom of your oven?

You didn't buy all-purpose flour, you probably bought SELF-RISING flour. Nah, Nah!

Was the bread in a drafty place during the rise? That's why its 2" inches thick in the bottom of the bread pan. Was the oven at a stable temperature or still coming up to temperature?

Where you in a hurry?

Tossed the half-raised dough into a much hotter oven?

Hmmm, that's why it's lopsided, cracking-upward, and slanting off-to-one-side.DO NOT BE DEFEATED! You can do it, apply your intellect.

Solve the Problem! Be Patient, Master it!

Many of my junior priests and priestesses have mastered the art and went on to teach their students and so on.

Bread making talk has become kind of a secret handshake in our lineage.

Rule 8

- Buying 30 books about Magick won't help you if you don't read the BOOK, I assigned you

Whenever I've engaged new magick students, there were certain things that I did from a practical viewpoint. I wanted them to have proper starting materials. I don't charge tuition for teaching; any materials came out of my own pocket. I came to see this giving as an offering to the universe and a first giving of myself to the student.

Every student I have ever had received a copy of Starhawk's book **"The Spiral Dance."**

I found that the book gives a sound basis for the goddess practice. Also, it shares an elegant philosophy for rituals within. If carefully used, a student could effectively be a solitary practitioner or even start a circle/coven using the book, especially if they read it a few times.

In 30 years of group practice, I have had several hundred students. Every one of them was given a copy of Starhawk's **The Spiral Dance**.

Some students quit and gave their books back, and we recycled them with other students. Perhaps another 50 also received a copy of Raymond Buckland's book **"The Complete Book of Witchcraft."** But the bottom line was everybody got a copy of The Spiral Dance.

What always annoyed me were the students who went out and started buying more and more books on the witchcraft and magick.

I told them to "Use what I give you for the first year or two and then invest in other books."

But there were always a couple of students who hit the New Age bookstores with an unquenchable thirst for more and more books about magick and witchcraft.

My joke has always been: *The witch who dies with the most books wins!*

The drawback was that, sooner or later, a tiny number of students contradicted me at every turn about technicalities, rituals you name it, always quoting some other author.

Several adepts and I concluded that because somebody published a book, they must be more of an expert than us.

As none of us had published a book of magick, so obviously we must be idiots deserving to be contradicted by the written words of published craft authors.

But the paradox was that most of these book hoard students; it seems we're trying to get to the bottom-line-of-magick, or in other words, they were looking for the proverbial shortcut.

Magical practice is a lot like learning to play a musical instrument. You don't buy a piano and take a dozen lessons and voila, overnight your concert pianist.

Too many people think magick is about lighting a couple of candles, burning some herbs, and chanting some mystical verbiage and presto you have a cause-and-effect miracle.

Nah, Nah, Nah, it doesn't work like that. I like to refer to magick is an **Art, Science, and Lifestyle**.

Okay, the debunkers reading this might agree that it's an art and for sure a lifestyle but dig their heels in and argue that it's not a science.

These folks think that one should be able to perform magickal experiments and give repeatable results. The problem is magick has all the quirky characteristics of quantum physics.

The truth is sometimes the act of just casually thinking about an action in a focused way makes it happen. Yet if we try and repeat it, we find that conditions have changed. <u>In essence, we the magickal adept have also changed</u>.

In quantum physics, just observing the state of an object or an effect changes it. So too; magickal practice sort of works in the same way.

A classic lesson I've had said to me by several of my teachers: ***"Don't even speak it if you don't intend for it to happen."***

So, let's get back to books. Why shouldn't you use multiple

books while the novice training?

If I teach you to make bread, a.k.a. magick; a certain way and instead of using my script/spell, you use parts of another or utterly different recipe/spell your results will be unpredictable.

If I tell you to use fast yeast and Aunt Betty's book says to use cake yeast, and you use Betty's yeast. I cannot predict the results.

So, if I give you a book to study from, it only makes sense that I expect my students to use it and not jumble the message by quoting other teachers and at least not while being a novice. After a year and a day, do as you wish!

A note to those magickal debunkers who all want repeatable science like magickal experiments. Remember this, Magick like bread making takes acquired skill!

Finally, consider "That no two loaves of bread will turn out the same way." The same goes for magickal workings, "No two executions of a magickal working will turn out exactly the same way."

Rule 9

Use all mundane methods first, only use magick to give the effort an added extra kick

I knew a gal once who did this huge ritual to make a wish for a musical recording career to take off. She wished for 10 hit albums and money.

The problem here is the literal aspect of magick. Wishing for a specific thing; versus the causes for the path for the eventual outcome.

What's remarkable was that a few weeks later someone gave her 10 CDs of hit artists. Likewise, about the same month, she received a significant dividend check from her insurance company quite unexpectedly.

From my point of view, her spell worked precisely as specified. This is clearly an example of the **principle of literal magic**.

In magick, specifications are everything!

If you are an artist, it's essential to do all the hard work of honing your skill in the desired profession or vocation. Magick comes into play when you're trying to get a break.

The break might be an audition with an agent. It might be a job interview with the producer. It might merely be an appointment with an influential person in show business.

Here's an example: I know a performance artist who had put together this really good comedy standup act. She tried for weeks and months to get an appointment with an agent who dealt with standup comics, but she couldn't get past the hardened secretary in his office.

She worked a ritual to get an appointment, just an appointment to pitch her act. The next day she made another attempt to make a telephone call for an appointment. As luck or magick would have it, the secretary was out running errands, and the agent himself answered his own phone.

She pitched herself and landed an appointment. The agent like her material but told her he couldn't use her. The comic in question went home rejected but happy that she'd gotten an appointment for the audition. When the comic got home, there was a voicemail waiting. It turned out to be from a colleague of the agent. While the agent she auditioned couldn't use her, he put in a good word about her with his colleague, who arranged for another audition for her to show her stuff, and she landed a comedy circuit booking. This is magick at its best!

Another example: Back in the late 1980s and early 1990s, I was trying to get a cable television show about Witchcraft launched. You must understand that in that era, the public's view of witchcraft was still very much "It's all black magic and witches are bad people."

I approached several Cable access television stations with a proposal for me to produce a cable series about what real witchcraft was about. Time after time, I kept getting doors slammed in my face. Finally, with humility and conviction, I pitched the president of a cable station in Virginia.

It was a hard sell, but at least she listened to me. She had considerable reservations but gave me a small contract for a measly six episodes as a summer replacement. If I had stomped away in a hissy-fit, I suspect that I would have probably never gotten the chance to tell the witchcraft story. I smiled and accepted the six-episode contract and happily signed the contract. I assembled a content and production team, and over the next few springtime months, we taped the six episodes for future play sometime during the summer.

Shortly afterward, a lady came to my door and told me that I needed to call the cable station because something had happened. I didn't have a phone at the time, so I walked to a convenient store and used a payphone to call the station.

The station's staff producer told me that a 300-word Associated Press story had gone out on the wires earlier in the day about my as yet untelevised program. I asked him what the problem was. That's when he told me that CBS and ABC news were sitting in the lobby, <u>and they wanted to talk to the Witches!</u>

Suddenly and inexplicably, national and international media visibility was raining down upon the obscure little

Virginia cable station.

In the weeks that followed, the cable station's president gave me a pair of thirteen-week contracts to produce the witchcraft-oriented program. Over the next two years, we received additional contracts, as well as an award for television excellence.

Ultimately, we produced about 70 of 30-minute witchcraft talk shows. The host and I granted over 80 media interviews in the two-year time frame of the program. All done with the focused <u>intention</u> of helping to change the negative narrative and image of witchcraft.

My team and I were all talented television people, and we all knew our trade, this was the mundane aspect.

The ***magical kick in the pants*** was a magickal working for "media visibility," which was performed on the holiday of Ostara, a classic fertility holiday and rite. Again, this was magick at its best.

Rule 10

Never bind another person

Of all my rules, <u>this is the most serious</u>. There's a principle in magic that what you send out, most especially if unjustified, can usually rebound back upon you threefold. Be warned never bind someone with magic.

Case in point, I know a man who had a rumor started about him that he was a serious misogynist.

I knew him to be a bit awkward around women, and all too often, he said the wrong things, and ladies were frequently very annoyed with him.

One summer, a lady got very outraged at him for making an honest pass at her. Enraged, she ranted to her gal friends, witches all.

And before you know it, all of them were wound up and decided to fix the man's wagon. The five of them went into the woods and did a serious binding spell. The nature of which was that he would never find the love of his life on till he changed his ways.

I guess none of these young priestesses had ever heard of pastoral counseling or intervention or perhaps buying the man a cup of coffee and talking to him about his manner. Instead, they chose to be judge, jury, and punisher.

This spell was worked about 30 years ago if my memory serves.

The man in question met the woman of his dreams a year or so later. You're happily married for a bit over 20 years until he had an untimely stroke and passed away.

The five priestesses had success in their careers, but none of them ever found the love of their lives. Each of them is now a middle-aged spinster. This is what we call in the magical trade as a significant magical blowback.

Be warned never bind someone with magick!

Rule 11

Never pray for the demise of your enemies

This goes in the category of **"Don't do Hostile Magick!"**

1st: Casting against others is against Wiccan Law! It's the Law.

<u>Oh? You're not Wiccan!</u> Then go ahead and ignore this principle at your own risk.

2nd: Never do magic in a hostile state of mind or in a hateful fever.

If you do hostile magick, especially in a hateful fever, you risk unintentional collateral damage. If you do hostile magick, you most certainly risk a magickal rebound because you weren't justified, and the universe knows it. To my students, remember what I said about magickal blowback.

Working magick in a hateful state of mind is not appropriate and, most undoubtedly, sloppy. Add to that there is an overriding ethics issue, namely, "who appointed you judge, jury, and punisher?"

Many of my early magickal teachers recommended that you wait for at least one moon cycle before considering hostile magick.

The idea is to give you a chance to cool off and think about your grievance and whether it's worth your time and trouble to attack someone that you are just upset with or that you believe did you grievous harm.

Attack magick or right or wrong shouldn't be done in the heat of the moment. But instead, it should be done cooled off, clear of mind, and well thought out.

Not to mention well-crafted and well-executed. In other words, attack magick must be premeditated. Am I encouraging this sort of action? Absolutely not!

One of my most excellent teachers preferred the approach of the "nice day wish."

The Principal

Wish the jerk a lovely, joyful, abundant day or perhaps an abundant month. Maybe he or she really needs it.

If he or she doesn't deserve it, the rebound is happiness for you. But let us consider that what they really needed was a break. A nice day or a nice month might be a positive turning point for them.

On the other hand, if the person in question is really a dyed in the wool jerk, the universe will abundantly ripen his or her karma, and that will be that.

That is the philosophy for what <u>I call little-fish-hostiles</u>.

Let's take a moment to consider the drug cartel lords, the terrorist masterminds, the very public so-called really evil people, <u>the big-fish-hostiles</u>.

Is it your responsibility to take these big bad guys out? In a word, NO! That's karma's responsibility.

You're not *Captain Magick* going after the nasties.

You are little more than a <u>magickal vigilante, plain and simple.</u> Get your damned ego out of it!

But what about the really big fish the Bin Laden's and the Saddam Hussein and guys like Kim Jong-un?

I like the approach of "No place to hide!"

Here is the spell-concept and philosophy of

"No place to hide!"

> **Incantation theme:** "May his injustices be dealt with by the greater right of the universe!
>
> May his sins and karma against humanity be ripened in the light of righteous examination.
>
> May he/she find no place to hide from his sins and karma. Bring him justice!"

The concept here is to ripen his karma and bring the power of providence raining down upon him, especially if the authorities-of-man can't.

{ *"No place to hide!" Inspired from the 1930s church gospel song by Dorothy Love Coates "No Hiding Place"*}

Rule 12

Never use magick to attract money, you might not like where it comes from.

In the 40 plus years that I've been involved with magic. The most common request that comes from non-magical folks and beginner students are for money spells and love spells.

MONEY SPELLS

In my early Catholic upbringing, I saw many traditional household spells, where a dollar or a five-dollar bill was put under the statue of the Virgin Mary. Actually, there's nothing wrong with that method of folk magic. To be honest, it's tried and true. Why?

Explanation: The statue of the Virgin Mary is symbolic of the Great Goddess, and the currency script placed underneath is very visual; therefore, symbolic both excellent tools for communicating with the Younger self. In magick, the more symbolic and less verbal you can make your altar or spell artifacts, the better!

The issue of money comes down to two issues greed and need.

Greed is by far the worst reason to work magic! Why? Magick has a price, think of it as a karmic price. A money spell by its very nature is driven by causes to manipulate a physical item. The money has to come from somewhere.

A lady I knew wished for half a million dollars. A few weeks later, she was involved in a serious industrial accident and the settlement about half a million. She lost a limb arm and will never walk unassisted again. Was it worth the price?

A teenager I knew wished for a boatload of money. She received the money as the insurance beneficiary when her parents were killed in a car wreck.

On the other hand, a wish for bona fide need is something else altogether. A wish for the resources to deal with the financial situation is less invasive.

A lady I used to know wished for the resources to deal with the house she inherited from a recently deceased mother. A home required severe repair. The wish for the resources was not a wish for money. As it turned out, she was approached by a house flipper to fix up the residence, and both her and the house flipper made a tidy sum.

I knew a man was concerned about a great deal of money he needed to send his kids to college; it was a costly school. He did a working for the resources to send his kid to university. As it turned out, two things happened: his kid changed his mind and decided to go to a much cheaper state school, and dad was promoted at work with a substantial raise in pay.

Never ask for the money. Instead, ask for the resources!

LOVE SPELLS

Love spells are messy, in my opinion. Even when done well, the results can be ambiguous.

There are factors to consider, one of them is "time and season," Are you really ready to receive that love of your life? A personal example:

My spouse and I, forty years ago, would never have looked twice at each other, nor would we have given each other the time of day. Yet about 20 years ago, we, by chance, met at a party. Bam! Chemistry kicked in, and we became an item. We are each other's love of our life. Neither of us can look at previous spouses and companions and say the same about them. Those people I'd say only helped season us into the people we are now.

If you aren't ready for the love of your life, no amount of having them underfoot now will make them right until you are both karmically ripe.

Case in point, I knew a very straight-laced lady, in the legal profession, her life was empty for the "love of her life." Being a very talented magickal adept, she decided to take matters into her own hands and performed a spell working to bring the "love of her life" to her.

Her first mistake was serious consideration as to her specifications and filters in her ritual. The day came. She

51

did her working on the right day, within the right planetary hours. It was as exacting a ceremony as you might expect from a perfectionist attorney might write and execute.

The **first issue,** she considered herself a straight person and never thought of herself as gay. The **second issue,** in a word, it wasn't her time and season. Perhaps it was karmic, who knows for sure.

All these great men kept falling into her life, and not one of them resonated with her heart. She was in agony for nearly ten years. The only solace she had during all of this was a lady legal colleague whom she confided her deepest secrets and feelings. In the end, our heroine figured herself out, and the two women fell deeply in love and are now happily married.

Another adept of my acquaintance, a lady scientist who worked for a well-known government agency, was sick of not having a guy friend. One day she did do a working to bring a great guy into her life. In the days following her working, she told another priestess and me what she had done. We both asked her what her filters were. "No filters on the guys; I figured I'd just wade through them." I could only bite my lip in concern.

An hour later, we all went to the local metro subway stop, our lovesick friend was going ne way. My peer priestess and I went the other way. Being a Sunday, we all had a wait for our respective trains. During our wait, my friend and I watched in dismay as our lovesick friend was hit on by no less than twelve different guys. In the weeks that followed, she called me on the phone and lamented that "every geek in DC was finding her." Always set limits & specifications.

Rule 13

Weather magick

Weather magick done well, and for the right intentions is terrific!

Weather magick performed for ego or for reasonable comfort rarely turns out well.

For those reading this who do not believe in any of this magick, please feel free to move on to another chapter.

For the practitioner, I must state for the record that I've seen some impressive weather work, good weather work, and sloppy weather work over the years. Sadly, I've seen my share of "Oh my, what did you do?"

I knew a little girl who was a natural weather adept. She could call in a snowstorm like the Army calls in an airstrike. These were mini- snowstorms that only seemed to affect the square-mile or two around her parents' house; that in itself was truly eye-opening. Her parents, for years, logged all the school snow days she was responsible for. Please understand we are not talking about snow flurry.

No, we're talking about 6 to 12 inches of powder. In the few years that she ran in my witchy friendship circles, my nickname for her was the "Snow Queen."

One of my mentors, a Cherokee medicine guy, was a fantastic weather worker. In the late 1990s, I watched him punch a hole in a cloud cover. There was this hurricane off the mid-Atlantic coast. The cloud cover of the storm extended a few hundred miles from the eye which was out in the Atlantic. Several neighborhood children and I watched quietly as he chanted his prayers. All around the neighborhood, it was raining except for the block where his house was, where we were standing 10 feet away from him was the clear blue sky above.

Later in his house, we watched a recording of local DC area 5 PM TV newscast. The weather guy was showing Doppler radar in images of the cloud cover and pointed out the exception for this odd hole in the picture. I remembered the weatherman remarking

"That's interesting. Why is there a stationary clear spot over Silver Spring, Maryland?"

We all got a great laugh because we knew why. I learned my weather technique from Big Bear. I did not learn his Cherokee prayers.

For the record, I must say the method is what-this is about, not necessarily one man's prayers to the divine for Weather relief.

About a year later, there was an El Niño season; there was a severe rainstorm in the Washington DC area. The rain was coming down as if that was the monsoon season. The monastics of a Buddhist monastery were preparing for a special kind of fire puja or fire-offering.

The problem was the rain was coming down like someone had turned on a faucet. The monks in charge of the fire pit knew they could not start the fire in this sort of rain downpour.

An elder monastic knew of my skills and asked me to do something about the downpour. The request was simple: stop the deluge for 30 or 45 minutes so the monks could get a roaring fire going in the fire-offering pit.

In essence, stop the rain so the people could pray and make offerings. That is a legit justification.

I agreed to help out. I took a small bowl of rice and a large Tibetan shell horn out into the yard in front of the Temple. I blew my horn and offered prayers in Tibetan and made offerings from a small bowl of rice and began blowing the horn again.

About 10 minutes after my impromptu ritual, the rain broke to a light sprinkle. Once Again, this was reminiscent of Big Bear's working.

For above the Temple and monastery grounds was a clear whole in the cloud cover with and blue twilight sky and stars above.

About 45 minutes later, the fire was blazing. The clouds closed up over the temple grounds, and the rain started again. That was the successful part of the weather practice!

The lesson here is not to put loose conditions on your request prayer! <u>Always set specifications!</u> Don't end the prayer by saying something like,

"… And after the fire is bright and full, you can do as you wish…"

Nah, Nah, Nah, don't do this!

During our Buddhist ritual, there was rain, serious blowing wind, and the strangest lightning anyone had ever seen.

Another Buddhist nun-Magickal Adept leaned into me at one point and whispered, "What did you do?"

The next day I got a phone call from the Big Bear, and he asked simply if I've been working weather magick in the area of the Temple. Of course, I told him yes.

He gave out great belly laughter and remarked,

"I have never seen purple and green lightning before… What did you do?"

Later that evening we had a long talk over supper about setting conditions with particular parameters in weather rituals

Frankly, I knew better, but I felt the words and technical device from the elder and peer were constructive.

LESSON: Remember, no matter how old you are or how long you've been in the craft. We are always learning, and we are all <u>still students</u> of one degree or another.

Back to weather magick. A few weeks later, during that

summer, the rain started again while we were at a Wicca camping event. Two younger students wanted a weather magick teaching, I agreed.

The rules for governing Weather magick are strict: Weather magick can be done to:

- support the People's rituals,
- to protect the People,
- and to relieve the People's suffering.

Stopping the rain for training or convenience doesn't fit into those rules. I decided the lesson had to be a gentle one working within the boundaries of <u>weather divas</u>, not hard weather control rituals.

I told the students each to grab a large baking bowl and to get soap and shampoo. Since we were all witches and nudity weren't an issue.

We walked out into the rain and proceeded to soap up and effectively shower in the pouring rain. I told them to save shampooing for the last thing. By the time our bowls were full of rainwater, we had begun to shampoo.

It was then, predictably, as our heads were full of shampoo, it stopped raining. With our bowls of water, we rinsed our hair. Obviously, the weather divas have a sense of humor.

Let's talk about another tradition.

Let's say you're Asian Buddhist, and you approached his holiness the Dalai Lama and explained that your home province was desperate for rain. He most likely would refer you to the High Lama in the Orthodox tradition of Tibetan Buddhism. The Dalai Lama is a member of the reformed tradition.

The Orthodox tradition has deep roots. 1000 years ago, in Tibet, the shamanic tradition was very much in flower. Then Padmasambhava came from India and taught the shamans Buddhist dharma and theory.

In Tibet, the Orthodox tradition has its roots in both shamanic magickal culture, and the tradition was the first to receive Buddhist thought in Tibet. The shamans saw Buddhist thought is totally compatible with their practices. Buddhism brought with it an ethical structure that helped discipline magickal practice.

This doesn't mean that everyone who joins the modern Tibetan Orthodox tradition learns the art of magick. Absolutely not!

But if you study Buddhist thought and you learn to read between the lines, you can come to understand how delicate the fabric of reality is and how easy it is to manipulate it.

Remember: Reality is an illusion, and under the right conditions with the right mindset, the fabric reality can be bent and manipulated. This is what we teach in Wicca 101.

When I embraced Buddhist thought, I found a home in the Tibetan Orthodox tradition. Many of the shamanic mindset within the Tibetan Orthodox tradition, are quite good at massaging the fabric of reality.

But I must caution those of you reading this book, do not run out and buy up all the books you can about Tibetan Buddhism.

The things I have talked about regarding magick in that tradition requires a greater understanding of what they are teaching.

You simply won't find a book that discusses practicing magick. What you will find is a comfortable place to understand Buddhist dharma and, on the side, classic metaphysics and a little bit of quantum theory. But it's never published in the clear! No, you must read between the lines and understand the fabric of reality.

One of the most famous Tibetan lamas, who was adept at weather magick, was the late Lama Yeshe Dorje, his revered nickname was the "Rain Maker."

A word of advice: if you think converting to Buddhism will lead to classes and instruction in Weather magick, I guarantee you it won't. It will, on the other hand, teach you to quiet the monkey chatter in your mind. Quieting the chatter in your psyche is of vital pre-requisite for such practices.

Rule 14

Use magic ever so gently

Words and the thoughts behind them are potent. As a teacher to new students, one must be careful how you think of things in your mind and speak softly with words that call about change and manipulation of matters.

Have you ever seen a mobile made from Dominoes? One flick of a finger sets off a chain reaction that usually grows bigger and bigger.

While I was in the military, I learned the saying or a story.

For the loss of a nail, the shoe was lost

For the loss of a shoe, a horse was lost

For the loss of a horse, a rider was lost

For the loss of a rider, a message was lost

For the loss of a message, the battle was lost

For the loss of a battle, the kingdom was lost

How often do we hear news of the train wreck or car accident that was caused by a malfunction of a part that costs less than a couple of dollars?

Magick is always about <u>cause and effect.</u> If you can massage the causes, you can manipulate the resulting effect.

For years I have watched apprentice practitioners tried to produce a magickal effect; bright, loud, and full of whiz-bang-- like the special CGI effects we see in the movies.

I've tried to caution these students against what they are doing.

But I used to get dismissed as a busybody. These days I get blown off as a crazy old witch.

Please respect the wisdom and experience of elders, use magic ever so gently!

This goes double for those young practitioners of Chaos Magical practices.

The best magick is a gentle as a baby's breath!

Rule 15

I will teach you magick with informed consent. If you screw up, it's on you. I warned you!

This is the: "I told you so clause."

My eldest daughter, a seasoned adept, read a narrative I wrote about magick that I wrote many years ago.

She complained that I explained the magickal process so well that just about anybody could understand it. That's when she objected in no uncertain terms that I was giving away the store.

"You're passing out loaded shotguns to third graders," she said metaphorically.

I sat on the manuscript for several years, then reread it, and after doing so, I took in the back yard and poured charcoal lighter fluid on it and burned it.

Karma is an absolute law of the universe is. I know a lot of witches and pagans who don't believe in karma. I console them, and I reassure them that <u>karma believes in them</u>.

If I teach you serious-minded magic, you run the risk of seriously screwing up. Because I showed you, I personally run the risk of karmic backlash, the likes of which you cannot imagine. Therefore, I require my students to assume full responsibility for the magic they work.

You come to magick of your own free will. By this commitment and this reckoning, you also assume full responsibility for your magickal practice.

If you can't accept the responsibility for your magick!

DON'T PRACTICE MAGICK!

Rule 16

Don't whine about what you screwed up, suck it up and fix it

There's an old computer systems adage:

"To err is human; to really foul things up requires a computer."

In magical terms the adage goes like this:

"To err is human; to mess things up on an exponential scale requires badly executed magick."

A beginning student typically has this notion that magick is supposed to have bright flashes and whiz-bang like they see in the movies.

Real magick: Properly executed is as gentle as a baby's breath, merely a gentle nudge.

If you do a magickal working, you should observe what the result is. If you messed up, fix it. Notice I did not say if the result isn't to your liking person. Big difference

Example:

I knew a witch in upstate New York who had a major jerk of a boss. So, the witch figured he'd get his boss transferred to an out-of-state location. The working was successful. The boss was transferred to the mid-Atlantic HQ of the business. But in our age of global Internet connectivity, the jerk boss remained the manager of the upstate New York branch managing old New York folks from Baltimore. Plus, he picked up the responsibility for a similar function at several other facilities. In the end, the witch still the same boss, but the boss was just out of the state.

The magick worked perfectly, except that karma continued the relationship, so what is the lesson here?

There is sloppy magick, and there is good magick. There is also karma, which is potentially capable of undermining good or bad magick; trust me, it frequently does.

I have observed over the years that if karma is at the root of any significant variation in your magickal working, you won't be able to change the situation, no matter what. End-of-story!

Always, be careful and mindful of what you ask for

.

Rule 17

Be careful what you ask for, you'll probably will get it... eventually

There's a saying in magick; "All things happen in their own time and season."

Many magickal practitioners I've known never pay much mind to the effects of karma, as I stated previously. Nor do they pay attention to the temporal considerations as in time.

Temporal considerations I've found are a huge deal.

I'll use the example of Remote Viewing. It was discovered early on that if temporal specifications were not defined on the target card that the individual viewers on an-away-team would find themselves reporting data about the target site from different periods.

There's a classic example of an Army Remote Viewer reporting data on a Russian base during the cold war. He drew a sketch of the site with high accuracy. The intelligence agency who requested the RV session criticized the session's data because they had aerial photographs that did not show a particular man-made feature that the Viewer reported.

As it turned out, two things were discovered: 1: the target card didn't have any time specifications. 2: the man-made feature in contention was built two months later and showed up on later intelligence photographs exactly as the remote Viewer had illustrated it.

But let's say you specify a precise time that you want your magick to be effective. The other thing you really must consider is karma. The effects of karma frequently are a huge issue, as I have previously stated.

Karma can and does impact magickal workings. That's not to say; that what you were trying to accomplish won't happen. It's just going to happen when the karma ripens enough to allow all the causes to occur.

So, keep in mind: Temporal/time and karmic considerations when planning a working.

My last thoughts on the topic of temporal and karmic considerations.

I've chatted with practitioners who have sniffed at me when I try to teach this subject at Craft Gatherings. I usually hear a remark like: "Well, my kind of magick always works and is never impeded by anything."

To that remark, I say, "Baloney!"

Rule 18

There's no "little bit of working magick." If you're in for a dime, you're in for a dollar.

If you want to do some protection around your home or bedroom with a little sage and sea salt, that's fine. If you're going to put $5 under the Virgin Mary or your Goddess statue for increased prosperity, that's fine.

But the moment you consider performing a working, something that requires spell casting, it's an entirely different story.

I come from the school of thinking that "dabbling" without a commitment to the art of magick only leads to problems. If you don't make the commitment to clearly learn the mechanics of magick, you shouldn't be doing it. I'm not asking you to train up to be a world-class mage; I'm only saying that you need to make some commitment to clearly learn the basics and intermediate elements at the level you'll be practicing at.

Don't practice outside the boundaries of your training!

How often do we hear non-magickal people say, "Oh... you shouldn't be messing around with that magick stuff?"

Why do they say that?

Either they did something and did it very wrong, or they knew somebody else who did something magickally and screwed up royally.

The scenario usually goes; somebody needed something outside of the realm of mundane resources, so they get the idea that magick might be a solution. They go out and buy a book about spell casting and decided to solve their problem with a splash of homebrew magick.

It's like a first timer trying to make a loaf of bread. The beginner doesn't understand the subtle aspects of the ingredients or working the dough. They make compromises in the process, and the result is usually disastrous or at the very least disappointing. Also, this person's failure only serves to give the magickal practice a bad name.

If you are going to work magick, take the time to study up a bit and don't just sit down with a spell book and dabble. You are only asking for trouble! Consider yourself warned.

Lastly, learn to meditate, divine, and connect to the great consciousness. I've found that solutions come to you in mediation. Its wisdom that usually doesn't show up in popular books.

Rule 19

**"Magickal students learn best when their cell phones
are off or locked in their car."**

Long ago, 25-30 years ago, we used to unplug the phone
and turn on the answering machine in another room, not
within earshot of where we were holding our circle.

These days everyone walks around with cell phones in
their pockets and purses. The problem, as I see it, is that
when people are asked to silence their phones at movies,
presentations, or classes.

There are always some fools who think the silencing
request doesn't apply to them. Naturally at some tender
moment, or an intriguing discourse, someone's phone
rings, usually with the most obnoxious ring tone. Then
there is the texting, with the related buzzing and ding bells.

I have sat in a temple prayer room and had my meditation
interrupted by others in the quiet space. Their phones
abruptly rang or rattled on the prayer benches.

I've watched students sitting on meditation pillows in a perfect lotus position. Suddenly open their eyes and pull out their phone from a pocket beneath them.

The whole scene looked like they were sitting on a nest trying to hatch something. In any case, they disturbed me and the many others who were working at being at peace and one with the universe.

I think what pains me is that if you quietly speak to them about the rules of no phones in the prayer room or in class, they get all indignant or have a hissy fit. Most students apologized and complied. Some students have stomped out; others had to be asked to leave.

When I lived in the Washington, DC area, my questions about the phone justification in the temple or circle space went like this.

- Are you part of the White House?
- Are you in the National Security Community?
- Are you a physician on-call?
- Are you a volunteer fire-rescue person on-call?

Lesson: "You're not going to become a magical adept, a good witch, a mage or Jedi knight with a cell phone going off every five minutes in your pocket. So, turn off the phone completely, or lock it up in your car.

Rule 20

"The Secret, what happens in Magickal space, Stays in Magickal space!"

There nothing nefarious is going on in witch's circles and covens. So why is it a "big" secret?

Magickal-working-space and magickal-training-space can, at times, be like a doctor's office or a

Catholic confessional or a psychiatrist's couch.

Despite the popular myth that circles and covens* always do magickal workings while in sacred space. The truth is that for magickal practitioners, sacred space is many times an environment and an exercise in learning to be in harmony with each other.

This harmony theme is an ongoing work in progress that every monastic and mystical organization everywhere has to deal with, no matter what the brief system or tradition.

For Witches, the environment of a circle or of a coven is one of perfect love and perfect trust.

I've heard the somber bearing of people's deepest feelings in sacred space. Likewise, I've listened to the most profoundly personal information revealed.

Any issues that can impede the harmony of the magickal team must be worked out in a way that contributes to the peace of the great whole.

Traditionally a circle or coven is a family of upwards of 13 persons or perhaps fewer individual witches. Here's a rough structure of witch organization. The actual naming varies from witch tradition.

Solitary – an individual witch who technically practices alone. In theory, every witch is technically a solitary. Doesn't matter whether we practice with others from time. Fundamentally as solitaries, we practice by ourselves.

Gaggle – a very loose association of witches that get together to practice irregularly. Membership is usually based on a very open invitation basis.

Circle – a somewhat tighter group of witches that get together to practice regularly. Membership is usually based on an invitation basis, based on individual member discretion or group consensus.

Coven – a very tight group of witches, membership-based on group consensus, and a strict screening.

Clan – a more significant association of individual Circles or Covens. Usually, these are hive-off daughter circles and covens from an original mother group.

RULE 21
Initiation – like a fine wine, is not to be done before its time.

Initiation is customarily performed in a year and a day after the student starts training.

The idea is that the student will have witnessed a full cycle of the year and the eight Sabbats. Initiation is a Rite of Passage not to be taken lightly.

It's probably the most significant rite in your craft practice. What I'm about to say applies if you are being initiated into a group or performing a solitary initiation. Being initiated is a rebirth of sorts, and it shouldn't be entered into lightly.

When someone is initiated, it's flexible. It's not a hard-fast Wiccan law or unbreakable tradition that it MUST be performed in a year-and-a-day.

In reality, it's more of a guideline. Most students are typically ready to receive Initiation rites after the cycle of a year, especially if the priest or priestess has done their job of teaching and screening.

Note that I said <u>most</u> students. Some students choose not to take initiation after a year. These students usually have deep personal questions whether or not they are ready, and that's just fine. This usually amounts to the student talking their reservations out with the Wiccan clergy.

There are always a few students that don't demonstrate the expected behavior, wisdom, and what I call craft demeanor. Maybe they can't demonstrate that they have done the required reading or that they understand the reading material.

Sometimes they attend monthly classes, moon rites, and Sabbats and do just too much farting around before or afterward.

Hey, we've all gotten the giggles in a circle. We've all messed up the altar and dripped the ceremonial wine. It's not about that. Sometimes they just don't take their role in a ritual serious enough; perhaps they don't play well with others. Remember: Harmony is a big deal in covens and circles.

Once upon a time, there were two of us, both somewhat seasoned solitaries. We both had the opportunity to train in a coven style tradition. So, we humbled ourselves and functioned as acolytes. We that made every mistake you could make and then some.

Our training rituals were "chaotic" at best. We broke ritual form so often that the other trainees thought we were both undisciplined screwups and disapproved of us equally.

We heard later that they protested our involvement in the

group and recommended to the priest or priestess that we weren't suitable for Initiation and should be booted out.

At the Sabbat six weeks before a year and a day, the priest or priestess invited everyone to submit petitions for initiation.

These petitions were to justify why you were qualified, a statement explaining your aspirations in the craft, and of course, a polite, respectful request for initiation.

Everybody submitted a formal petition except my ritual partner and me. We both figured that we were the least likely to be accepted into one of the sponsoring circles, especially in light of the disapproving talk about the two of us.

As it turned out, unbeknownst to us, a senior member of one of the sponsoring circles wrote a petition letter on our behalf.

She made a case that we each had been to class faithfully and pitched in when extra hands were needed for set up or for after class or ritual clean up.

She further stated that our irregular and chaotic ritual style was akin to watching a couple of "ritual buffoons" or "crazy sacred clowns."

She made a case that our form style was simply that "our form."

All the elements of the ritual were carried out as required, just not by the proverbial book. Finally, she argued that a good reason why neither of us had submitted a petition was that we were both humble enough to know we weren't perfect. In the end, neither of us was invited to the initiation ritual with the other acolytes.

We were however in initiated in a separate circle a few weeks later, attended by only the elders of the clan.

Afterword

Are the preceding rules hard and fast? Of course not.

At best, they are a guiding philosophy as to what many other Witch Elders and I are looking for in a prospective student. Also, what we expect starting out and down the road.

Some of my peer witches think I'm a hard ass. But, many of my priest and priestess peers have similar conditions, some only dictate to students, some published as handouts.

At a minimum, these rules are a guideline to magickal craft friends and acquaintances who might refer prospective students to me and to me.

Upon first reading, some of you will come away with the opinion that I'm a hard ass, that's good, you got it right!

You should also take it to mean that I take the teaching of the metaphysical and magickal arts very seriously. I don't have time to fool around with students who decide to study magick on a whim or whose hearts aren't really in it or aren't willing to do the study work the art requires.

The magickal life is a very rewarding and a joyous one for those who have focus and are willing to bring balance to their lives.

In the final analysis:

Real Magick is about being in unity with the great universal consciousness.

Or to use a more modern mythological quote, **"Being one with the Force."**

Bright Blessings and Peace

Lady Tashi

High-Priestess of the Temple of Tara
www.TempleofTara.org
A Neo-Pagan Congregation serving Syracuse, NY and Central New York.

About the Author

Mundane Life

Cheryl Costa grew up in a small factory town in the northeast United States. She has been a social advocate for Transgender issues for over forty years. Her social activist papers will be archived at SUNY Albany.

Professionally, Cheryl is a retired career Aerospace professional in both Industrial filmmaking and Information Technology.

Vocationally, she's a published and produced playwright, a television producer, indie filmmaker, a talk radio host, and an internationally read journalist.

Metaphysically

Cheryl "Lady Tashi" Costa's grandparents on both sides of her family were metaphysically oriented and instilled in her, a sense of profound wonder concerning the spiritual, paranormal and mystical thought.

Cheryl was raised Roman Catholic but left that tradition at 17. In her mid-twenties, was introduced to Wicca while in the Navy and became a Wiccan solitary. In the 1980s, she evolved into a group practice and later began teaching.

Lady Tashi's craft practices have evolved significantly over the decades as her experience grew. In the late-1990s, she took a sabbatical from senior priestess duties.

During her "Walk About," she was introduced to Orthodox Tibetan Buddhism in the Washington, DC region and spent seven years in monastic life.

These days she considers herself a **Mystic Witch** and prefers to teach a <u>Nouveau Wicca style</u>.

As of this writing, she's a regular writer for **Wicca Magazine,** and she's a weekly talk radio host on KCOR in Las Vegas and discusses metaphysical topics on a program called, "**Cosmic Questions**."

As of this writing, she is the high priestess of the **Temple of Tara**, a Neo-Pagan Congregation in Syracuse, NY. **www.TempleofTara.org**

Lady Tashi lives in a quiet retreat with her wife Linda in Upstate New York.

Lady Tashi **does not** give out spells, perform workings, or do readings for strangers.

If you would like light craft-related correspondence with Lady Tashi, feel free to reach out to her at the following email: **LadyTashi@CherylCosta.com**